T66695   3/07   Capstone $22.60

WAR MACHINES **AIRCRAFT CARRIERS**

The Nimitz Class

by Michael and Gladys Green

Consultant:
Lieutenant Matthew Galan
Public Affairs Officer
Navy Office of Information, New York City

Capstone press
Mankato, Minnesota

Edge Books are published by Capstone Press
151 Good Counsel Drive, P.O. Box 669, Mankato, Minnesota 56002
www.capstonepress.com

Library of Congress Cataloging-in-Publication Data
Green, Michael, 1952–
    Aircraft carriers: the Nimitz class / by Michael and Gladys Green.
    p. cm.—(Edge books. War machines)
    Includes bibliographical references and index.
    Contents: The Nimitz in action—Inside the Nimitz—Weapons and tactics—The future.
    ISBN 0-7368-2720-X (hardcover)
    1. Aircraft carriers—United States—Juvenile literature. 2. Nimitz (Ship: CVN-68)—Juvenile literature. [1. Aircraft carriers. 2. Warships. 3. Nimitz (Ship: CVN-68)] I. Green, Gladys, 1954– II. Title. III. Edge books. War machines.
V874.3.G7423 2005
623.825′5—dc22   2003027971

Editorial Credits
Katy Kudela, editor; Jason Knudson, series designer; Molly Nei, book designer;
    Jo Miller, photo researcher; Eric Kudalis, product planning editor

Photo Credits
Corbis/Yogi Inc./Robert Y. Kaufman, 29
DVIC/PH1 Dave J. Cummings, 11; PH1 Ken Brewer, 18–19; PH2 Tracy Lee
    Didas, 17
Fotodynamics/Ted Carlson, 6
Getty Images Inc./Sandy Huffaker, 5
U.S. Navy photo by JO2 David Valdez, 21; Naval Sea Systems Command, 24–25;
    PH1 Michael W. Pendergrass, cover; PH2 Andrea Decanini, 12; PH2 Chad
    McNeeley, 7, 9; PH3 Christopher B. Stoltz, 13; PHAN Jason Frost, 15;
    PHAN Konstandinos Goumenidis, 23; PHC Johnny Bivera, 27

1 2 3 4 5 6 09 08 07 06 05 04

Table of Contents

CHAPTER 1

The Nimitz in Action

A U.S. Navy Nimitz class aircraft carrier floats on the ocean. Dozens of planes wait on the flight deck. Many of these Navy planes carry bombs under their wings. The planes' pilots need to find enemy trucks. These trucks are carrying supplies to enemy forces.

The Navy planes are big and heavy. The carrier's flight deck is short. The planes need help to take off. Before takeoff, each plane hooks to a catapult. The catapult pulls the plane forward. This pull helps the plane gain enough speed to take off.

A Navy jet fighter takes off from an aircraft carrier's flight deck.

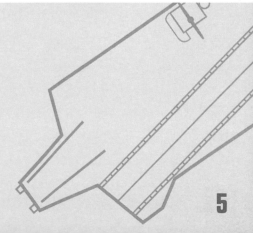

LEARN ABOUT:

Navy jet fighters

Short runways

Nimitz history

An aircraft carrier's flight deck is shorter than an airport runway.

One by one, each plane leaves the carrier's flight deck. The Navy pilots quickly find the enemy supply trucks. Bombs drop from the planes. The trucks explode. The Navy pilots have done their job. They fly their planes back to the carrier.

Landing a plane on the carrier's small flight deck is tricky. As each plane touches down, its tailhook catches a cross-deck pendant, which is also known as a wire. Four wires cross the landing area on the flight deck. After the plane stops, the tailhook releases the wire. The flight deck crew then directs the pilot to park the plane.

Wires on the flight deck stop a plane after it lands.

Nimitz Class Carriers

The Navy named its Nimitz class aircraft carriers after Admiral Chester Nimitz. Work on the first Nimitz class carrier began in 1968. The USS *Nimitz* entered Navy service in 1976.

The newest Nimitz aircraft carrier is the USS *Ronald Reagan*. The Navy began using this ship in July 2003. It is the ninth Nimitz carrier. The last carrier in the Nimitz class will be the USS *George H. W. Bush*.

The Navy believes its aircraft carriers are its most important weapon systems in service. Carriers are almost always on the move. They are much harder to find and destroy than land targets are.

A jet fighter plane lands safely on the USS Ronald Reagan.

CHAPTER 2

Inside the Nimitz

The Nimitz class carriers are the largest warships ever built. The ship's hull, or body, is 1,092 feet (333 meters) long.

Decks divide a carrier into sections. Each deck has many rooms. Crew members use these rooms to sleep, eat, and store equipment. A carrier's top deck is the flight deck.

The Carrier Island

A large steel tower stands on the flight deck. The crew calls this tower the island. Crew members inside the island steer the ship. They also direct the planes on the flight deck.

A room called the bridge is at the top front of the island. The ship's captain directs the actions and movements of the ship from the bridge.

The carrier island has seven floors, including the bridge.

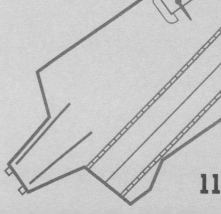

LEARN ABOUT:

Design

Crew duties

Carriers' power source

Primary Flight Control, or Pri-fly, is also located on the top level of the island. The Pri-fly area extends over the ship's flight deck. The crew can see everything that is happening on the flight deck.

An experienced Navy pilot, called the air boss, manages the crew in Pri-fly. The air boss directs the actions of the planes on the flight deck. The air boss also directs the planes within a 5-mile (8-kilometer) area of the ship on a clear day.

Crew members in the Carrier Air Traffic Control Center help track a carrier's planes.

The crew in the Combat Direction Center directs planes in battle.

Air Traffic Control

The Carrier Air Traffic Control Center (CATCC) has several rooms below the flight deck. The CATCC crew directs the aircraft to the carrier. They make sure the planes land safely.

The Combat Direction Center (CDC) is next to the CATCC. The CDC crew directs planes in battle.

Building a Ship

Many materials are needed to build a Nimitz class carrier. These materials include about 60,000 tons (54,500 metric tons) of steel. The average carrier also includes about 500,000 tons (450,000 metric tons) of aluminum. Builders also use about 900 miles (1,450 kilometers) of cable and wiring.

Builders install a great deal of equipment on a carrier. A carrier has nearly 30,000 lights. A carrier also holds 2,500 phones and 3,000 TVs. Equipment also provides the crew with fresh water each day.

Hangar Deck

The hangar deck holds many of the carrier's planes. Four elevators are located around the edges of the flight deck. Crew members use the elevators to move planes between the flight and hangar decks.

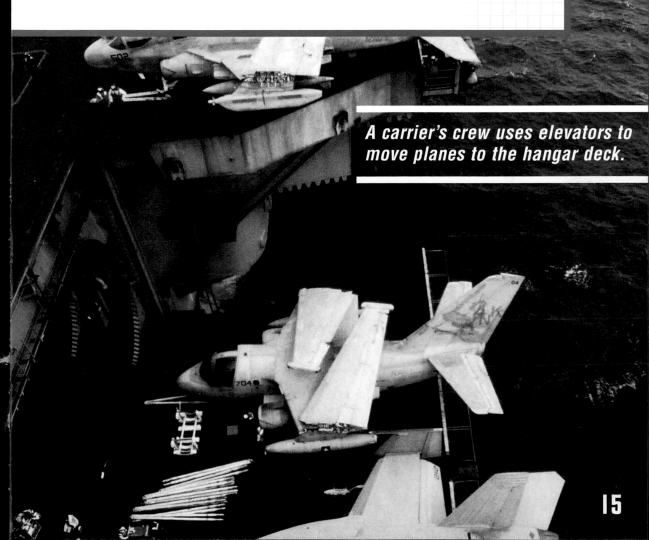

A carrier's crew uses elevators to move planes to the hangar deck.

A carrier's planes are stored and fixed on the hangar deck. The ship's crew also stores fuel tanks and other equipment on this deck.

Power Plant

Nimitz class carriers are nuclear powered. These aircraft carriers can last about 20 years without adding fuel.

The Nimitz has two nuclear reactors. These nuclear reactors produce heat and create high-pressure steam. This steam transfers to generators that produce electricity for the ship.

Steam turbine engines turn the ship's four large propellers. The propellers can push the carrier to a top speed of 35 miles (56 kilometers) per hour.

Crew members repair planes on the hangar deck.

The Nimitz Class

Function:	Aircraft carrier
Manufacturer:	Northrop Grumman Newport News
Date First Deployed:	1976
Length, overall:	1,092 feet (333 meters)
Flight Deck Width:	252 feet (77 meters)
Power Source:	Two nuclear reactors
Top Speed:	35 miles (56 kilometers) per hour
Aircraft:	85
Crew:	5,680

1   Hull

2   Island

3   Flight deck

4   Catapult

5   Landing area

CHAPTER 3

Weapons and Tactics

An aircraft carrier's most important weapons are its planes. An aircraft carrier's planes are the first weapons used as a defense against an enemy attack.

A Nimitz class carrier can carry up to 85 planes. There are six different kinds of aircraft on a carrier. Each type of plane has its own separate mission.

Nimitz carriers are equipped with other weapons. They carry guns and surface-to-air guided missiles.

Other Navy boats and ships help protect aircraft carriers. Submarines and warships find and destroy enemy submarines.

Planes are an aircraft carrier's most important weapons.

LEARN ABOUT:

Gun systems

Missiles

Navy support

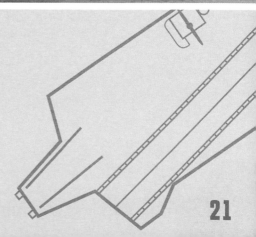

Air Defense Gun System

The Navy has gun systems on its Nimitz aircraft carriers. These gun systems shoot down antiship missiles. New gun systems can also serve as antiaircraft guns.

One of the new gun systems is the MK 15 Phalanx Close-In Weapon System (CIWS). Antiship missiles fly too fast for a person to shoot down. The MK 15 Phalanx CIWS computer can find antiship missiles. The weapon system takes only two seconds to spot a missile. It then shoots down the missile.

Air Defense Missile System

Newer Nimitz carriers have a short-range air defense system. This system is the MK 29 RIM-7M Sea Sparrow. It includes eight surface-to-air guided missiles. These missiles can blow enemy missiles or planes out of the sky.

Crew members on a Nimitz carrier load ammunition into a Close-In Weapon System.

Carrier Strike Group

The Navy sends smaller warships to sea with aircraft carriers. These warships help protect the carrier. The Navy calls the warship combination a carrier strike group.

A strike group includes an aircraft carrier, attack submarines, and warships. The warships and attack submarines protect the carrier from enemy submarines. The warships can also shoot down enemy planes or high-speed missiles.

The U.S. Navy has carrier strike groups stationed around the world.

CHAPTER 4

The Future

The Navy's newest Nimitz carrier will be the USS *George H. W. Bush*. This ship is the Navy's 10th Nimitz class carrier. It will also be the last carrier added to the Nimitz class.

The USS *George H. W. Bush* will have updated equipment. The ship's island will have updated navigation and communication systems. The carrier will also have new aircraft launch equipment. A new fuel system will make it easier for the ship's crew to store and handle aircraft fuel.

The USS *George H. W. Bush* will enter Navy service in 2008. It will be the most advanced ship in the Nimitz class.

Former President George H. W. Bush looks at a model of the USS George H. W. Bush.

women of the United States Navy...
rica safe in the century ahead as they
ntury now coming to a close."

George Herbert Walker Bush
Forty-First President
United States of America

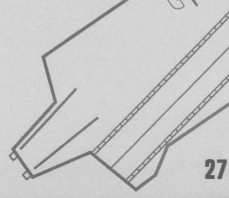

LEARN ABOUT:

New Nimitz carrier

CVX 21

Carrier updates

Future Plans

The U.S. Navy is planning a new class of carriers. The Navy's code name for these carriers is CVX 21. Northrop Grumman Newport News plans to begin construction of the first CVX 21 class carrier in 2007.

The Navy has not decided the final design of the CVX 21. The design will be based on experiences with the USS *George H. W. Bush*.

The U.S. Navy continues to improve its current warships. Each new Nimitz carrier is an improvement over the last. The Navy also updates each carrier when it comes in for service or repair.

Nimitz carriers will continue to be important ships for the U.S. Navy.

Glossary

bridge (BRIJ)—a room where the captain controls a ship

catapult (KAT-uh-puhlt)—a device that helps launch aircraft off the flight deck

flight deck (FLITE DEK)—the top deck of an aircraft carrier; planes use the flight deck to take off and land.

hangar (HANG-ur)—a large sheltered area where aircraft are parked and maintained

hull (HULL)—the main body of a ship

island (EYE-luhnd)—the area on a carrier's flight deck where the captain and crew operate the ship

missile (MISS-uhl)—an explosive weapon that can fly long distances

propeller (pruh-PEL-ur)—a set of rotating blades that provides thrust to move a ship through water

turbine engine (TUR-bine EN-juhn)—an engine powered by steam or gas; the steam or gas moves through the blades of a fanlike device and makes it turn.

Read More

Beyer, Mark. *Aircraft Carriers, Inside and Out.* Technology—Blueprints of the Future. New York: PowerPlus Books, 2002.

Cooper, Jason. *U.S. Navy.* Fighting Forces. Vero Beach, Fla.: Rourke, 2004.

Doyle, Kevin. *Aircraft Carriers.* Military Hardware in Action. Minneapolis: Lerner, 2003.

Internet Sites

FactHound offers a safe, fun way to find Internet sites related to this book. All of the sites on FactHound have been researched by our staff.

Here's how:

1. Visit *www.facthound.com*
2. Type in this special code **073682720X** for age-appropriate sites. Or enter a search word related to this book for a more general search.
3. Click on the **Fetch It** button.

FactHound will fetch the best sites for you!

Index